The Solar System

By Kris Hirschmann

World Discovery Science Readers™

SCHOLASTIC INC.

New York • Toronto • London • Auckland • Sydney
Mexico City • New Delhi • Hong Kong • Buenos Aires

More stars are visible in areas away from city lights, as seen in this view of the night sky in the Arizona desert.

Chapter 1

Looking at the Universe

Our planet seems very big to us. But it is really just a tiny speck floating through space. Space plus everything in it is called the **universe**. The universe is so big that it would take a beam of light at least 20 billion years to travel from one end to the other!

Light travels at a speed of 186,000 miles per second (297,600 km per second). It takes about eight minutes for the sun's light to reach Earth.

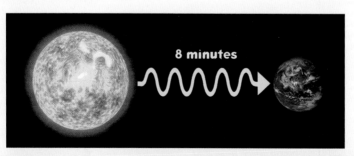

8 minutes

Scientists think the universe was born between 10 billion and 15 billion years ago. Most scientists believe that the universe started with the **Big Bang**. This event was like a giant explosion. It created huge amounts of dust, gas, and other materials. Over billions of years these materials clumped together into stars, planets, and all the other things we see in space. One of these planets was Earth.

These colorful specks are actually pictures of distant galaxies taken by the Hubble Space Telescope. These galaxies were formed during the Big Bang.

The Big Bang pushed matter outward very quickly. Today the effects of the Big Bang are still occurring. Matter in the universe is still moving away from the original explosion point because its force was so great. This is why scientists believe the universe is expanding. Scientists also think that someday the matter will stop moving out and start being pulled back with help from a force called **gravity**.

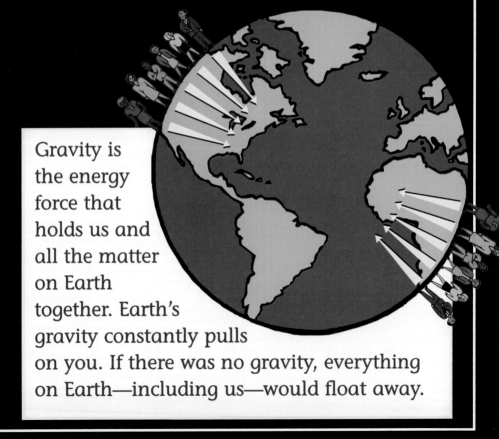

Gravity is the energy force that holds us and all the matter on Earth together. Earth's gravity constantly pulls on you. If there was no gravity, everything on Earth—including us—would float away.

From its orbit around Earth, the Goddard Space Flight Center's Cosmic Background Explorer (COBE) captured this edge-on view of our Milky Way galaxy in infrared light.

Galaxies are the building blocks of the universe. A **galaxy** is a group of stars and planets that travel together through space. Scientists believe that the universe contains about 125 billion galaxies. Each galaxy contains hundreds of millions of stars.

Different galaxies have different shapes. Some galaxies are shaped like spirals. Others are shaped like round blobs. Some have no regular shape.

Our galaxy is called the Milky Way. It is a spiral galaxy, and it contains between 300 billion and 500 billion stars.

The closest galaxy to the Milky Way is called Andromeda. Andromeda is about 2 million **light-years** away. This means it would take a beam of light 2 million years to travel from Andromeda to the Milky Way.

Earth is in one of the Milky Way's spiral arms, near the galaxy's outer edge.

A bird's-eye view of our solar system

You can see thousands of lights in
the night sky. Most of these lights are
other stars in the Milky Way. Some might
be planets. Some might even be galaxies.
The galaxies are so far away that they
look like small, bright blobs.

The Little Dipper and the Big Dipper are two well-known constellations.

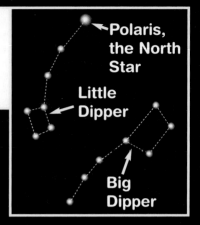

Polaris, the North Star
Little Dipper
Big Dipper

Stars and galaxies sometimes seem to form patterns; some look like crabs, or hunters, or bears. These imaginary "space pictures" are called **constellations**. Many constellations were named before 2000 B.C.E. by Babylonian astronomers. The ancient Greeks added more constellations around 150 C.E.

There are 88 named constellations. Twelve of these constellations are called the signs of the Zodiac.

Aries—one of the twelve signs of the Zodiac

Mercury

Venus

The nine planets of
our solar system

Earth

Mars

Jupiter

Saturn

Uranus

Neptune

Pluto

Chapter 2

The Solar System

Our "neighborhood" in space is called the solar system. The solar system includes our sun plus everything that **orbits**, or revolves around, it. The main orbiting objects are the nine known planets: Mercury, Venus, Earth, Mars, Jupiter, Saturn, Uranus, Neptune, and Pluto.

An imaginary line called an **axis** runs through every planet. A planet spins around on its axis. It is daytime on the part of the planet that faces the sun. It is nighttime on the part of the planet that faces away from the sun.

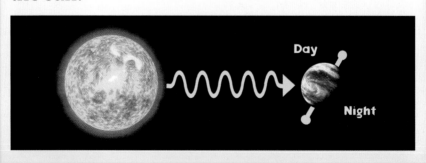

Day

Night

The sun is at the center of the solar system. The sun is big and very, very heavy. In fact it contains about 99.8 percent of all the matter in the solar system. You could fit more than a million Earths inside the sun!

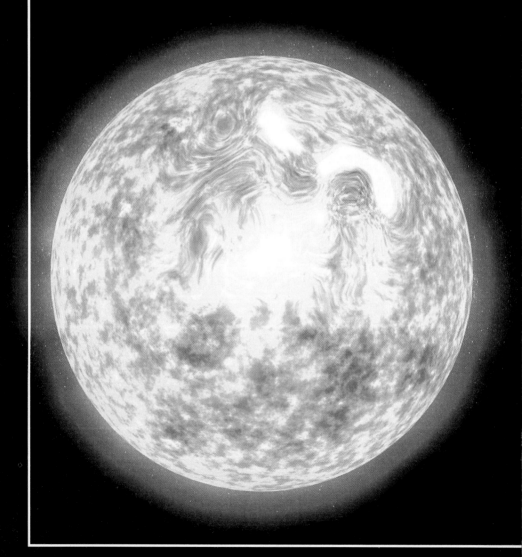

The sun is a **star**. This means it is a hot ball of gas. The temperature in the sun's core is about 27 million degrees Fahrenheit (15 million degrees Celsius). The heat and light made by the sun travel through space in all directions. Some of the sun's energy hits Earth. The sun's rays make our skies bright and give us warmth.

The sun's gravity holds planets, comets, asteroids, and all the other things in our solar system. Without the sun's pull, these things would drift off into open space.

One full orbit of a planet around the sun is called a year. The length of a year is different from planet to planet.

Planet	Year Length
Mercury	88 Earth days
Venus	225 Earth days
Earth	1 year
Mars	1.9 Earth years
Jupiter	11.9 Earth years
Saturn	29.5 Earth years
Uranus	84 Earth years
Neptune	165 Earth years
Pluto	248 Earth years

The four planets closest to the sun—Mercury, Venus, Earth, and Mars—are called the **inner planets**. The inner planets are small and rocky.

The *Mariner 10* space probe's first image of Mercury on March 24, 1974

Mercury is much smaller than Earth. It travels faster than any other planet in the solar system. It zips around the sun at a speedy 30 miles (48 km) per second.

Venus is surrounded by clouds made of acid. These clouds trap the sun's heat. The daytime temperatures on Venus can reach about 900 degrees Fahrenheit (480 degrees Celsius)! Venus is the hottest planet.

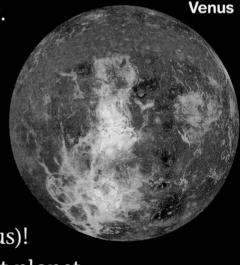

Venus

Earth is our home. It is special because it is the only planet in the solar system with oceans of water. It is also the only planet that is known to support life.

Earth

Mars

Mars is sometimes called the "red planet" because it is covered with reddish-brown soil and rocks. Space probes have landed on Mars and sent back pictures of rocky deserts.

Earth's axis is tilted. This tilt creates seasons. Different parts of Earth are tilted toward or away from the sun at different times of the year. Parts of Earth that are tilted toward the sun have summer weather. Parts that are tilted away from the sun have winter weather.

Fall in the north

Summer in the north

Winter in the north

Spring in the north

The five planets farthest from the sun are called the **outer planets**. Jupiter, Saturn, Uranus, and Neptune are made mostly of gas and are called the **gas giants**. Pluto, the solar system's outermost planet, is small and rocky like the inner planets.

Jupiter is the solar system's biggest planet. Its surface shows stripes of colored gas. One feature, the Great Red Spot, is actually a giant hurricane three times as big as Earth!

Saturn is best known for its colorful rings. The rings are made of millions of floating rock and ice chunks.

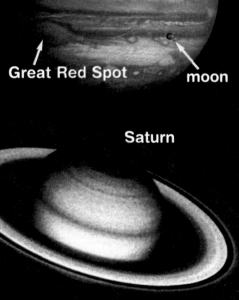

Jupiter, its Great Red Spot, and one of its 61 moons

Great Red Spot

moon

Saturn

Uranus is a beautiful blue-green color all over. This planet travels on its side. Its axis is horizontal, not upright like that of the rest of the planets.

Neptune is a stormy planet. Winds blow as fast as 1,500 miles (2,400 km) per hour through Neptune's atmosphere.

Pluto is the smallest planet. It has an unusual orbit. Sometimes Pluto crosses inside Neptune's path and becomes the eighth planet for awhile.

Most of the planets in the solar system have **moons**. A moon is a natural object that orbits a planet.

Earth	1 moon
Mars	2 moons
Jupiter	61 moons
Saturn	31 moons
Uranus	27 moons
Neptune	13 moons
Pluto	1 moon

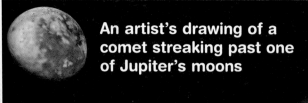

An artist's drawing of a comet streaking past one of Jupiter's moons

What's the Difference?

OBJECT	MADE OF	FOUND
Comet	Dust, rocks, ice, frozen gas	Irregular orbit around the sun
Meteoroid	Rocks and/or metal	Anywhere in the solar system
Asteroid	Rocks and/or metal	The asteroid belt between Mars and Jupiter

Chapter 3

Comets, Meteoroids, and Asteroids

The nine planets of the solar system are not the only objects orbiting the sun. Comets, meteoroids, and asteroids are also trapped by the sun's gravity. These objects are an important and interesting part of our solar system. Sometimes they can even be seen from Earth. Watch for shining objects zipping across the night sky. You just might be seeing a meteor!

The gassy envelope around a comet is called the **coma**. The nucleus is in the center of the coma. A comet's trail is called the **tail**.

Nucleus

Tail

Coma

Comets are large balls of dust, rocks, ice, and frozen gas. They have irregular orbits. A comet passes very close to the sun at one end of its orbit. The other end of the orbit may lie near the outer edge of the solar system.

Comets are cold and dark most of the time. But a comet starts to heat up when it gets close enough to the sun. It gives off a trail of water vapor, gas, and dust. Light from the sun reflects off the trail and makes it easy to see.

This picture shows a comet's orbit. The tail always points away from the sun.

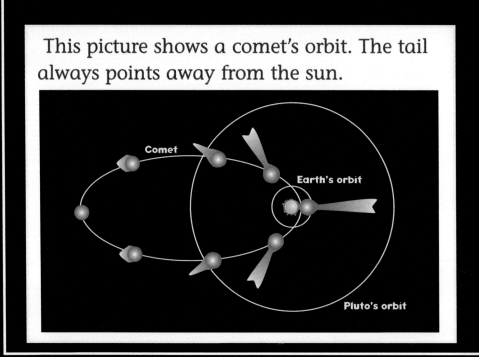

Comet

Earth's orbit

Pluto's orbit

Comets take many years to orbit the sun. Halley's Comet, for example, makes one orbit every 76 years. Comet Hale-Bopp, which could be seen from Earth in the spring and summer of 1997, will not appear again for more than 2,000 years.

In 1994 a comet called Shoemaker-Levy 9 rammed into the planet Jupiter. Fireballs rose nearly 2,000 miles (3,200 km) from the planet's surface after the comet pieces struck. Could this ever happen to Earth? It's possible. But it is not likely to happen any time soon. None of our solar system's known comets is heading for Earth.

This photo shows Hale-Bopp, the most recent comet visible from Earth.

Meteoroids are rocks or metal chunks that float around in the solar system. They do not have orbits. Most meteoroids are very small.

Sometimes meteoroids enter Earth's atmosphere. Then they are called **meteors**. Meteors heat up as they move through Earth's air. They get so hot that they start to glow. Glowing meteors are easy to see as they shoot across the night sky.

A meteor streaks through the outer edge of Earth's atmosphere.

A lot of meteors burn up before they hit the ground. But some make it all the way to Earth's surface.

Barringer Meteorite Crater near Winslow, Arizona

Then they are called **meteorites**. Large meteorites leave deep holes, or **craters**, when they land. One big crater is found in Arizona. It is .75 mile (1.2 km) wide and 600 feet (180 m) deep.

Meteorites have made many craters on the Earth's moon.

Asteroids are rocky objects that orbit the sun. Most asteroids are found between Mars and Jupiter in a band called the **asteroid belt**. The asteroid belt probably contains millions of asteroids.

The biggest known asteroid is named Ceres. It is about 580 miles (930 km) across. Other large asteroids are Pallas and Vesta, which both measure about 340 miles (550 km) across. But these asteroids are giants. Most asteroids are much, much smaller.

An artist's painting of the asteroid belt

The asteroid belt probably contains about 40,000 asteroids that are more than 0.5 mile (0.8 km) across. The rest are much smaller.

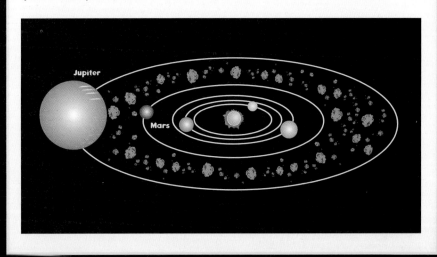

Scientists think that most meteors were once asteroids. The asteroids became meteors when they got loose from their orbits and began floating freely through space.

The asteroid belt is like a bunch of leftovers. It contains most of the matter that didn't get used to create the solar system's planets and moons. Objects in the asteroid belt take between three and six years to orbit the sun.

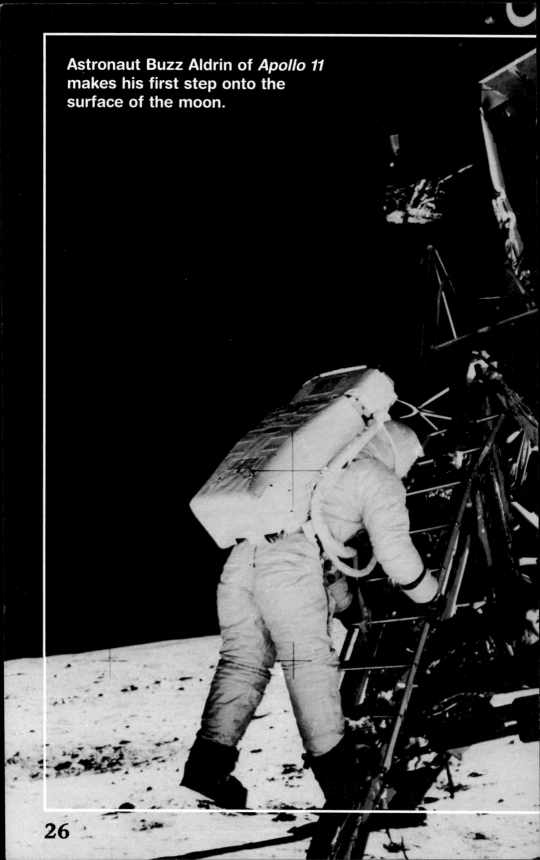

Astronaut Buzz Aldrin of *Apollo 11* makes his first step onto the surface of the moon.

Chapter 4

People in Space

Are we alone in space, or could there be life elsewhere in the universe? No one knows the answer to this question. But scientists are trying to find out. They have been sending rockets, satellites, telescopes, and even people into space for the past fifty years. They hope that someday they will find signs of life beyond Earth.

Scientists have identified more than sixty planets outside our solar system. Stars with planets have wobbly paths. Stars with no planets travel in a straight line.

Scientists have many ways of studying space. The easiest way to study space is to look through a **telescope**. The best telescopes are the ones that are sent into space on rockets. Space telescopes can "see" better because they do not have to look through Earth's **atmosphere**. The Hubble Space Telescope, for example, has taken exciting pictures of distant galaxies and other things in the universe.

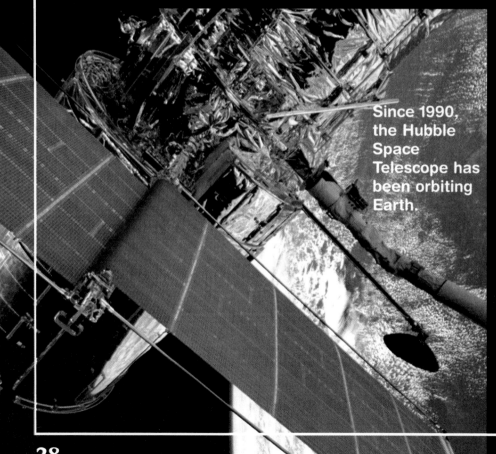

Since 1990, the Hubble Space Telescope has been orbiting Earth.

Probes are another way to study space. Probes are rockets that fly to faraway places. One space probe called *Voyager 2* traveled all the way to Neptune. This trip took about twelve years. *Voyager 2* flew past Neptune and took some amazing pictures.

Sometimes people even visit space. These people are called **astronauts**. Astronauts have walked on the moon. Some astronauts have lived in space for many months aboard space stations. They do scientific experiments while they are there.

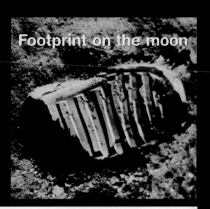
Footprint on the moon

Voyager 2 and its sister probe, *Voyager 1*, are still traveling. Soon they will leave the solar system. Scientists hope these probes will keep sending information back to Earth for many years.

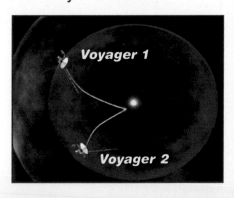
Voyager 1

Voyager 2

Some scientists think life might have existed on Mars at one time. They think this because Mars has dried-up lake basins and riverbeds. If Mars had water, it might have had living things, too.

Two **rovers** landed on Mars in early 2004. The rovers' mission was to study rocks for clues about ancient water on Mars. Scientists are still studying the information sent back by these machines.

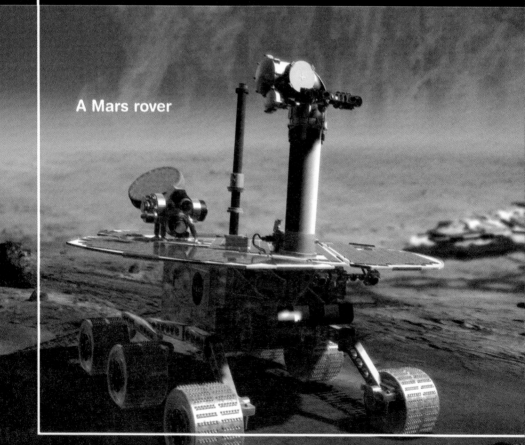

A Mars rover

No one knows if the Mars rovers or other space probes will find signs of life in the universe. But scientists will keep trying. There are millions upon billions of stars in space. It would not be surprising to find living creatures near some of these stars. Even if scientists do not find life, they are sure to learn many new and fascinating things about space.

The Mars rovers were attached to balloons when they landed. The balloons let the rovers bounce instead of crashing.

Glossary

Asteroid: Small rocky object that orbits the sun.

Asteroid belt: A region between Mars and Jupiter where most of the solar system's asteroids are found.

Astronaut: A person who journeys into space.

Atmosphere: The envelope of gases surrounding any natural object in the universe.

Axis: An imaginary line around which a planet spins.

Big Bang: A giant explosion that most scientists believe started the universe.

Coma: The gassy envelope around a comet.

Comet: Orbiting ball of dust, rocks, ice, and frozen gas.

Constellation: An imaginary picture in space made by "connecting the dots" between stars.

Crater: A mark made when a meteorite hits a planet's surface.

Galaxy: A group of stars and planets that travel together.

Gas giants: Big planets made mostly of gas. In our solar system, Jupiter, Saturn, Uranus, and Neptune are gas giants.

Gravity: A force that pulls objects toward its center.

Inner planets: The four planets closest to the sun (Mercury, Venus, Earth, and Mars).

Light-year: The distance a beam of light can travel in one year.

Meteor: A meteoroid that enters Earth's atmosphere.

Meteorite: A meteor that reaches Earth's surface.

Meteoroid: A rock or metal chunk without a regular orbit.

Moon: A natural object that orbits a planet.

Orbit: To revolve around a central object.

Outer planets: The five planets farthest from the sun (Jupiter, Saturn, Uranus, Neptune, and Pluto).

Probe: A space vehicle that is sent to explore a distant area.

Rover: A space vehicle that lands and travels on another planet or moon.

Solar system: The sun plus everything that orbits it.

Star: A ball of gas that gives off heat and light.

Tail: The dusty trail left behind by a traveling comet.

Telescope: An instrument that makes distant objects appear closer.

Universe: Space and everything in it.